User Stories Applied
For anyone new to Agile

By Andrew R. Brien

Copyright © 2018 Andrew R. Brien

All rights reserved.

ISBN: 1986164748
ISBN-13: 978-1986164740

DEDICATION

For my father, Ray.

CONTENTS

	Acknowledgments	i
1	Introduction	3
2	Why Agile is Different	7
3	The Big Picture	21
4	User Stories	27
5	Estimating	43
6	High Level User Story Workshops	47
7	Template User Story Cards	49
8	Image, figures and tools library	59
9	Agile Dice	61
10	Glossary	65
11	Index	71

ACKNOWLEDGMENTS

I'd like to thank the following project professionals who have helped me understand the Agile process.

Agile Coaches; Shane, Andrew, and Carl

Project Managers; Ashley, Durjoy, Brad, and Patrick

Business Analysts; Aaron, Amanda, Ashley, and David

Experience Designers; Dan and Kat

1 INTRODUCTION

I know there's a lot of information available on Agile Project management and User Story writing. I noticed that the information overload had many people unsure of where to start. So, I created this guide to help you get started and move beyond the theory and hype.

This Is Not a Book You Read—It's a toolbox for you to use

This book is meant to be a building block in creating an understanding of how to actually get started with Agile and User Stories. I'll cover the basics and provide you with details of where to find more information. There are tools, worksheets, and examples, use them, cut them out of the book, copy them and change them so they meet your needs.

Write all over this guide, highlight, underline or cross out, in short, get started and try!

Some assumptions I've made

I'm assuming you're in an Agile team, and that you need to quickly get an understanding the core concepts of writing User Stories. You don't really have time for all the theory and just need a quick formula to get started. I'm assuming you've had some training or have done some research on the topic. If not that's OK but you may need to read up a little, I'll provide you helpful links for that.

There are in my opinion three types of agile practitioners:

- The **Agile Evangelist** - everything must be done using Agile! All ceremonies must be completed without question. There is a correct way of doing Agile and they know it!
- The **Agile Cowboy** - agile is the best option because I don't need documents anymore! I'll do anything I like and just say it's an Agile practice. I don't even follow the basics!

- The **Agile Optimist** - that's me! I'll take the core parts of Agile and apply them as they are needed, I will bend some rules and break some but ultimately I'll be faithful to the core.

You may have met the Agile Evangelist and Cowboy types in the past and it's left a bad taste in your mouth! I understand that. It's OK to feel a little uncertain about this new framework and using User Stories for your requirements. If you're lucky you will have an agile coach and get some training, but ultimately the best thing you can do is just get started. It's OK to make mistakes, in fact, it's one of the quickest ways to learn! Hopefully, this guide will help you avoid the really basic ones!

This guide is intended for all roles in an Agile team and in fact stakeholders and management as well. No matter if you are the Scrum Master, Developer, Tester or Product Owner the tips in this book will be helpful.

I've learned the hard way, this guide is full of my personal thoughts, beliefs, and behaviors. I'm hoping you will be able to take what I've learned and apply it, remember I'm an Optimist! Adapting and learning are core functions within Agile, I expect you to adapt and change. Use this guide as a starting point.

Before we look at User Stories in detail I'll take you through the basics of the Agile Framework. It's important you understand the framework and the core practices.

To assist you understanding how Agile works I've developed the below simple visual, it's based on my experience which is mostly in Scrum.

Figure 1.01 – Agile Big Picture Overview

Now in most "how to books" you get great little diagrams and images that really help to explain concepts, it would be great if you could have copies of the images! Well as I said this is not a book you read! All the images including the photos are available for you to download.

The images are in the PNG format for use in PowerPoint and Word. You can edit the SVG files or print the PDF copies. All the diagrams are open sourced or created by me!

Look for the document reference number it's based on the chapter number so the above image is 1.01 – Agile Big Picture Overview.

So, you can change the diagram to better meet your needs like this:

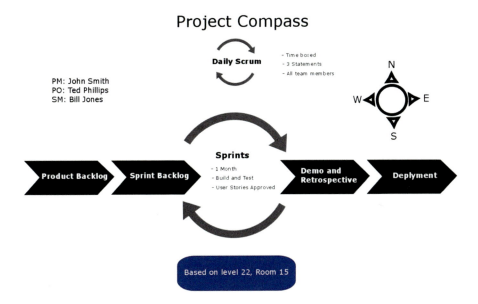

It's really easy to add your own terminology, project name, and methods.

Andrew R. Brien

2 WHY AGILE IS DIFFERENT

While it might take a little time for teams and stakeholders to see the benefits of using Agile, they quickly become apparent. Agile projects consistently run smoother with better results produced.

Agile is at its core simply a way to manage projects. It can be used for virtually anything, but it was founded in the world of software development.

In this guide I focus on general agile projects, my personal experience has mostly been in software development for large financial companies. It's important to understand that the core principles can be used in any field.

Agile breaks down larger projects into small, manageable chunks called sprints. At the end of each sprint (which generally takes place over a consistent time interval) something of value is produced. The product produced during each sprint should be able to be put into the world to gain feedback from users or stakeholders.

This is the core difference between Agile and Waterfall project management. In Waterfall, you have a sequenced process.

So you don't start any building work until you gather all the requirements, you then start the design, and don't start development until the designs are signed off on.

With Agile you have business analysts, developers, testers and business people working together simultaneously.

Here are the top five reasons I think Agile rocks:

Speed to Market or Early Delivery of Business Value

Agile lets you get your product in the hands of your users as quickly as possible. During every sprint, an Agile project delivers something of value. At any point, you may determine you want to release what has been delivered. This means you can start building a user base or test a hypothesis early.

It also means that you can stop the project at any point. You may find that the first release delivered enough business value. And that doing more work will have a marginal improvement result.

Better Risk Management

Incremental and regular releases mean that the product can be used early and by users compared to Waterfall delivery. This lets the team identify issues and feature defects early in the process, therefore avoiding costly "Change Requests". Agile is accepting of change and this adaptability means it isn't a problem when the scope has to change midway through the project.

Here's a little graphic that shows a comparison of Waterfall and Agile, it shows the reduction in risk when a release occurs early in the process.

	Project Team				Time →					
Waterfall	Design Team	Design/Requirements								
	Build Team					Build				
	Test Team								Test	
	Project Team					Time →				
Agile	Design Team	Sprint 0	Sprint 1	Sprint 2	Sprint 3	Release One	Sprint 4	Sprint 5	Sprint 6	Release Two
	Build Team									
	Test Team									

Figure 2.01 – Waterfall vs. Agile

We can also say that the constant delivery of business value at the end of the sprints reduces the delivery risk. Why? Because we have delivered early we can change direction quickly resulting in a better product.

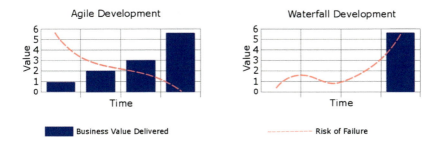

Figure 2.02 – Agile vs. Waterfall: Risk vs. Business Value Delivered

When we look at releases its clear the Agile development process allows for the business to adjust the product being built. The business often thinks they know what they want:

2.03 – What the Business Wants

In Waterfall projects, often they don't get it:

Project Starting Point

2.04 – What the Business Gets – Waterfall

You see things change. What the Business wanted three months ago is not what they now want. Waterfall does not cope well will change. Agile on the other hand with frequent releases can offer the Business the opportunity to change course:

Project Starting Point

2.05 – What the Business Gets - Agile

It's more flexible

Agile embraces change. The principle of "responding to change over following a plan" is considered by many as a core strength of Agile. Projects and software projects more specifically consistently change. As a product is created and comes to life or the market changes, the business should be able to react and update the product to meet the new needs of the users. Agile also realizes that requirements are emergent; they develop over time. Some great ideas are bound to come along mid-project, so having a locked down scope doesn't work. By embracing change Agile lets stakeholders and teams take advantage of these opportunities.

Cost Control and Failing Fast

Unlike traditional projects, an Agile project is flexible around scope. What often happens during a project is that the client (aka the business) realizes the original features they wanted no longer meet the user needs. Then there is the opportunity to fail fast! With a traditional project, you first create a lot of complex documents and spend as much as 30% of the budget before you start to build the product.

Then you discover there is a technical issue that makes the project impossible to complete. As opposed to Agile where you will find the same technical issue within a few sprints, meaning you can stop spending money on an impossible project much sooner. This allows the business to change direction. Launch a different solution much sooner and pay less. But what if you need to stick to a budget? No problem! Agile projects can rearrange their product backlog so that critical or new features are implemented at the expense of less important features, not your budget.

Transparency

When I walk into an Agile Project space I'm hit with Big Information Radiators; better known as task and project boards. It's all there for you to see, taste and feel! There are no compartments or silos, the team works together, in the same space with the same goals. Because Agile uses sprints you see progress in short time frames! Because releases are frequent you get feedback from users and stakeholders during the project. Working software/functional outcomes are the primary measure of success.

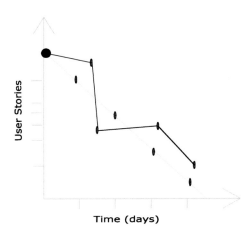

Figure 2.06 – Burn Down Chart

But what is Agile exactly?

Agile is an umbrella term for a group of project delivery frameworks and methods.

It is a way to manage the delivery or build process of a project. You can apply Agile to virtually anything, but it was founded in software development.

Basically, Agile breaks down larger projects into small, easily managed chunks called sprints. At the end of each sprint, something of value is produced. The product produced during each sprint could be put into the real world (into "production").

Unlike other delivery methods which are strictly sequenced (here's a Waterfall example; Business Requirements, Functional Design, Technical Design, Development and finally Testing). Agile has designers, developers and business people working together simultaneously.

While there are a number of delivery methods that loosely fit into Agile, the main thing to remember is that Agile is a Framework, not a sequenced methodology.

What I've found is there are a number of core features and processes that should be applied to all Agile Programs. Ultimately, it's up to individual teams on how to apply them.

Agile is a journey, not a destination!

Figure 2.07 The Agile Umbrella

Industry bodies and Organizations

Agile is an umbrella term for a group of project delivery frameworks and methods. There is no single industry body. I've listed below some of the organizations that actively support the Agile Community.

Agile Alliance

Agile Alliance is a global non-profit organization dedicated to promoting the concepts of Agile software development as outlined in the Agile Manifesto.

https://www.agilealliance.org

Agile Business Consortium

The Agile Business Consortium is a non-profit organization seeking to develop business agility. Their website holds a lot of information on the Dynamic Systems Development Method (DSDM).

https://www.agilebusiness.org/

International Institute of Business Analysis (IIBA)

The IIBA is the leading global industry body for Business Analysts. It provides comprehensive training around requirements gathering. The Business Analyst Body of Knowledge (BABOK) provides a lot of details around how User Stories can be written.

http://iiba.org

Large Scale Scrum (LeSS)

LeSS is an umbrella concept allowing for Agile to be scaled to enterprise levels. It is considered a 'lightweight' framework.

https://less.works/

Project Management Institute (PMI)

PMI is the leading global industry body for Project Managers. It offers comprehensive training for Project Managers working in Agile environments.

https://www.pmi.org/

Scaled Agile

The Scaled Agile Community supports the development of SAFe and provides members resources, training, and certification.

http://www.scaledagileacademy.com

Scaled Agile Framework (SAFe)

SAFe is an umbrella concept allowing for Agile to be scaled to enterprise levels. It is modular, allowing an organization to apply it in a way that suits its needs.

http://www.scaledagileframework.com

Scrum Alliance

Scrum Alliance is the leading organization that encourages and supports the widespread adoption and effective practice of Scrum.

They offer certification and resources to practitioners.

https://www.scrumalliance.org

The International Consortium for Agile

ICAgile offers knowledge and competency-based certifications in Agile practices.

https://icagile.com

SCRUMstudy

SCRUMstudy is an accreditation body for Scrum and Agile certifications.

http://www.scrumstudy.com

SPOTLIGHT - Test and Learn

The Agile Framework allows projects to release working software quickly. This allows the project to see how the end users react to new features. The second benefit is the business receives some value sooner.

For example, the first release provides the customers with new functionality, the business also gains valuable sales.

The second release provides a better and more complete user experience.

Getting early and relevant feedback allows you to change direction quickly. Agile embraces change! If we discover the customers don't like something we remove it! If you find out they really like something we expand it!

THE CORE OF AGILE IS THE MANIFESTO

Agile as a framework was made popular by the "Agile Manifesto":

AGILE VALUES:
INDIVIDUALS AND INTERACTIONS OVER PROCESS AND TOOLS
WORKING SOFTWARE OVER COMPREHENSIVE DOCUMENTATION
CUSTOMER COLLABORATION OVER CONTRACT NEGOTIATION
RESPONDING TO CHANGE OVER FOLLOWING A PLAN

PRINCIPALS:

We follow these principles:

- Our highest priority is to satisfy the customer through early and continuous delivery of valuable software.
- Welcome changing requirements, even late in development. Agile processes harness change for
the customer's competitive advantage.
- Deliver working software frequently, from a couple of weeks to a couple of months, with a
preference to the shorter timescale.
- Business people and developers must work together daily throughout the project.
- Build projects around motivated individuals. Give them the environment and support they need,
and trust them to get the job done.
- The most efficient and effective method of conveying information to and within a development
team is face-to-face conversation.
- Working software is the primary measure of progress.
- Agile processes promote sustainable development. The sponsors, developers, and users should be able to maintain a constant pace indefinitely.
- Continuous attention to technical excellence and good design enhances agility.
- Simplicity-the art of maximizing the amount of work not done- is essential.

- The best architectures, requirements, and designs emerge from self-organizing teams.
- At regular intervals, the team reflects on how to become more effective, then tunes and adjusts
its behavior accordingly.

Agile understands that projects are inherently unpredictable. We should expect changes and be able to manage it. Agile focuses on the high-value features and priorities everything.

For more detail see the Agile Manifesto web site (http://www.agilemanifesto.org/).

While Agile has a clear set of values and principles it's not a formal methodology. I've now worked in three financial institutions who would say they run agile development shops. In each institution, Agile was applied differently in many ways.

Core Agile Practices

Product Backlog

The list of requirements or User Stories

Backlog Grooming

Keeping the Backlog relevant, detailed, estimated and PRIORITISED

Planning

Select User Stories to be build in the Sprint

Sprints

Time boxed development 2 to 4 weeks

Daily Stand-ups

Daily team Status Report

Showcase/Demo

Demo WORKING software

Retrospectives

End of Sprint continuous improvement review meeting

Figure 2.08 Core Agile Practices

While Agile is a framework, meaning you can add or subtract steps as needed, if you're not doing all of the practices then you are on the fringes of Agile, not the core.

For example, in all three institutions, I have worked in that claimed to be "Agile" we used Users Stories, Project Walls, Stand-ups, and Sprints. The differences were in the methods of documentation (including using software to track User Stories), showcases, retrospectives, co-location of staff and length of the individual Sprint.

Other differences were; Stand-Ups were not compulsory daily, User Stories were not always in the "As a… I want… So that…" format and retrospectives were different in terms of who attended and what was discussed.

Here are some of the other major practices:

Focusing Statement:
- A short statement defining what the project is all about.

Success Sliders:
- Success Sliders give the team a shared understanding around how the project will be managed. The elements used can vary but generally are based on five considerations. Scope, Cost, Time, Quality and Team Satisfaction.

Social Contract:
- A team agreement on how the team will interact internally and externally. It is effectively the values the team will use to run the project.

User Persona:
- A fictional character that represents a user of the end product, such as a customer.

Epics, Features and User Stories:
- Lists of functionality that will be delivered written using the "As a… I want… So that…" formula.

Definition of done:
- The project teams list of requirements to be forefilled before the User Story can be defined as complete.

Estimation:
- The process undertaken by the team to estimate the effort to complete each individual User Story.

Sprint Planning:
- The process undertaken by the team to determine which User Stories will be built in each Sprint.

Co-location of team members:
- Having your core team in one place.

Project Walls:
- Usually a Story Wall/Sprint Wall, a Design Wall, and a Project Wall

Burn Up Progress:
- A chart that shows how many User Stories have been completed and how much of the budget remains.

Release Planning:
- The planning process undertaken to manage the User Stories across the planned releases.

Technical Practices
Below are some of the technical practices that can be applied to Agile.
  Pair Programming:
  - Where two or more developers work together on the same code.

  Technical/Business Spikes:
  - Proof of concept reviews undertaken quickly to determine if the concept can be used during the project.

  Design Lead Development:
  - CX (Customer Experience) or UX (User Experience) Sprints in which customer testing is undertaken to determine the best solution.
  - CX/UX continues to be part of the sprints adding to the design.

  Test-Driven Development:
  - The testing process that relies on short test cycles either automated or manually with rapid feedback to developers.

  Automated Testing:
  - The process and tools that allow for automated testing, including regression testing.

MISCONCEPTIONS

I've heard a number of misconceptions from people who really don't understand Agile like:

IT'S UNPREDICTABLE - Agile can be unpredictable at times as it embraces change. But all projects are unpredictable and have to manage change. It is impossible to know exactly what your end users want. Agile embraces this unpredictability and leverages it to produce better results.

THERE'S NO DOCUMENTATION – In Agile we need to make sure that everyone understands the requirement. Hence the introduction of the User Story. A User Story is designed not to be a written requirement but a reminder to have a detailed conversation where everyone leaves with the same understanding. I would say that the average Agile Project creates the same amount of documentation as a traditional project, only its created as required and does not need to be in a formatted document!

IT REQUIRES MORE TEAMWORK - Agile demands collaboration between all core team members. I believe everyone loves to collaborate, it's much more interesting and fun. Yes, there is a bit more upfront work that needs to be done to get everyone on the same page. Then when you see the end results; a better product; delivered faster and for less money, you get happy users, stakeholders, and team members.

I've faced a lot of skepticism over the years. In my first Agile program we delivered a new end to end home loan management system:

- Under budget
- On time
- With three additional features

The waterfall team estimated the project would take 2 years, we took 18 months.

On my second major Agile project we:
- Completed 3 releases in 9 months
- New sales revenue started at 3 months
- We hit 120% of sales volumes in 9 months

The waterfall team estimated the project would take 1 year, with no possibility of a release in 3 months.

In both projects, we created full documentation, but not always before the sprint though!

3 THE BIG PICTURE

It's important to understand how Agile works. Sometimes it's a lot easier to explain a process using a diagram. And there are a lot of Agile diagrams out there! So, I've created a model that goes from very high level to low level.

You've already seen it in chapter 1. So, let's start with it so we get the process firmly cemented in your mind.

Agile, at its core, is really a 5-step process that constantly repeats;
1. Create User Stories and priorities then in the Product Backlog
2. Groom the User Stories, to improve the teams understanding and create the sprint Backlog
3. The sprint runs – use the daily stand-up to monitor the process
4. Demo the working product and have a retrospective of the sprint
5. Deploy the product (optional)

Figure 1.01 – Agile Big Picture Overview

Before you start building:

Product Backlog:
To create your Product Backlog, you need to:
1. Have a Vision – what do you want to achieve
2. Assign a Product Owner
3. Gain input from Customers and Stakeholders
4. Create your Epic User Stories, in prioritized order
5. Create Features and User Stories

Figure 3.01 – Create your Product Backlog

Vision
How do you create a vision?
There are a few tools you can use to build your vision.
1. The elevator pitch – write a 60-second speech on why the project is important
2. Product Vision Box – make a physical "breakfast cereal" box, write on it the core selling points and value adds.

Figure 3.02 – Vision Box

3. Who, why, what, when – simply list out the key facts
4. Onion chart – often used to confirm the stakeholders and the environment of the work

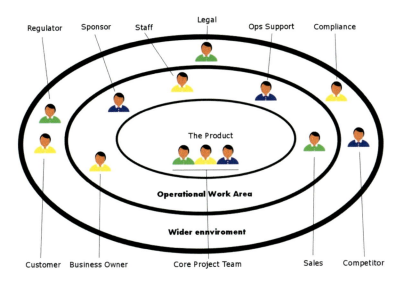

Figure 3.03 – Onion Chart

5. Lean Canvas – this process allows you to focus on problems, the solutions, key metrics and competitive advantages (see Spotlight "Lean Canvas" on page 26)

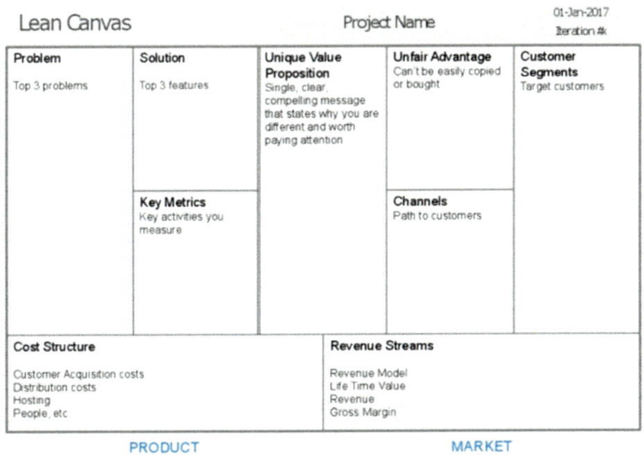

Figure 3.04 – Lean Canvas

6. Why and How Now vs. Why and How Future Model – a simple matrix; How the process is currently done, Why the process is currently done, How the process will be done in the future, Why the process is done in the future.

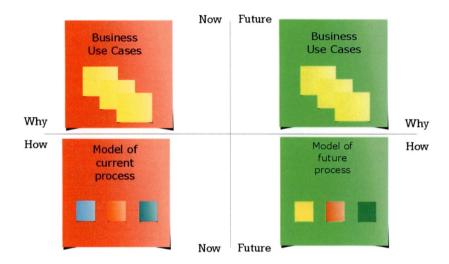

Figure 3.05 – Why and How Now vs. Why and How Future Model

7. SWOT (Strengths, Weaknesses, Opportunities, and Threats)

	Helpful	Harmful
	Strengths S	Weaknesses W
	Opportunities O	Threats T

Figure 3.06 – SWOT

Get Feedback from Customers and Stakeholders

Your Vision needs to be confirmed. The best people to do this are your customers and stakeholders. I've used the "Blast Off" workshop to ratify the project vision. At the blast off workshop, I invite; the principal stakeholder, a Subject Matter Expert, a Business Analyst and the applicable Tech Lead. At the meeting, I have the elevator pitch on the wall, a stakeholder onion chart and a context of work diagram. We then develop the other artifacts.

Figure 3.07 – Workshop group

Assign a Product Owner

A Product Owner is appointed. The Product Owner is the proxy "Customer" and is responsible for working with Stakeholders to define and prioritize the User Stories in the Product Backlog. It's a good idea for the Product Owner to be able to write User Stories.

Figure 3.08 – Product Owner

So now let's look at User Stories in more detail.

> **SPOTLIGHT – Lean Canvas**
>
> *Originally geared toward entrepreneurs, the Lean Canvas is designed to ask all the right questions to guide your thought process in uncovering your projects unique value proposition. The Lean Canvas helps you assess whether or not your project and it's business objectives has an advantage over your competitors.*
>
> *It's a big picture tool that really adds value to your project.*
>
> *Lean Canvas is an adaptation of the Business Model Canvas by Alexander Osterwalder which Ash Maurya created in the Lean Start-up. It promises an actionable and entrepreneur-focused business plan. It focuses on problems, solutions, key metrics and competitive advantages. For more information about the author of the canvas, refer to the blog post http://www.ashmaurya.com/2012/02/why-lean-canvas/*
>
> *You can try out the concept for free at https://xtensio.com/lean-canvas/*

4 USER STORIES

Why use User Stories?

Kent Beck came up with the concept of User Stories, he knew that the business requirements documents were failing. The simple reason being that written documents can be interpreted differently by different people. They result in a lack of shared understanding.

Figure 4.01 I'm glad we agree

Misunderstanding is only half the story, we may waste lots of time and money building what the document describes, only to find out that's not what the customer wanted!

User Stories get their name not from how they're supposed to be written, but from how they're supposed to be used by the team. If together we talk about the problem we're solving, who will use it and why then we can build a *shared understanding*.

Figure 4.02 I'm glad we actually agree

What is a User Story?

A User Story is a simplistic way of documenting the requirements and the desired functionality. The User Story will tell you three things about the requirement; **Who** requires it, **What** they need and **Why** they need it, this should be the benefit they are looking to achieve.

A good User Story is a complete task written in the voice of the user. They are short, simple and easy to understand statements.

Well-formed stories also meet the criteria set out by Bill Wake's in his "INVEST" acronym.

How do you write a User Story?

There is a general rule that the User Story is made up of three parts;
As a <type of user>
I want <function>
so that <benefit>.

SPOTLIGHT – INVEST

Independent
Negotiable
Valuable
Estimable
Small
Testable

Well-formed User Stories make life a lot simpler for everyone. Use the INVEST acronym to help you remember what makes up a good User Story. You can also use the "Magic Question" as part of the invest process. You should always ask "How will I know when we've done that?" In other words define some acceptance criteria for each User Story.

Independent - *We want to be able to develop in any sequence*

Negotiable - *Avoid too much detail; keep then flexible so the team can adjust how much of the story to implement*

Valuable - *Users or customers get some value from the story*

Estimable - *The team must be able to use then for planning*

Small - *Large stories are harder to estimate and plan. By the time of sprint planning, the story should be able to be designed, coded and tested within the sprint*

Testable - *Document acceptance criteria, or the definition of done for the story, which leads to test cases*

User Stories are all about a user, how they interact and what benefit they are looking for. Therefore, you should try to avoid generic user roles, create roles such as; customer, manager, call center operator etc.
Ideally, a User Story should be small enough to be analyzed, build and tested in a single sprint.

Figure 4.03 A Knight's User Story

Epics, Features and User Stories

Some user stories will be too large to complete in a single sprint; some are so large they represent almost all of the project.

These project-level user stories are commonly called "Epics". Epics are usually broken down into Features which again are too large to complete in a single sprint as well, but are much smaller than the Epic.

Features represent a major part of the epic. The features are broken down into User Stories which can be completed within the sprint cycle.

User Stories must be prioritized in the Product Backlog, this dynamic list is continuously updated because of reprioritization and new, updated, refined and sometimes deleted User Stories.

It may be easier to think of the problem as a boulder. A boulder is a really big rock. Moving a boulder is hard work. If you need to get a boulder to the top of a hill a simple strategy is to break it down. What you need to do is break the boulder up into smaller rocks, then take the rocks and break them into smaller rocks, finally break the small rocks into pebbles. It's easy to move pebbles to the top of a hill.

Figure 4.04 Taking a boulder up a hill

When you first start working with User Stories it will most likely be with the epic story. While you may be tempted to just drill down to the details first, it's more important to understand the big goal.

Once you understand the big goal you can start breaking it down into important subgoals.

User Stories Applied

Below is an example of how a project can use Epics, Features and User Stories.

User Story	Story Type	Details
As a Knight I want to slay the dragon so that I can save the princess.	Epic (Big)	This is the whole point of the project expressed in a single User Story.
As a Knight I want armuor so that the dragon won't eat me.	Feature (Medium)	Armour is key to protecting the knight, it's a Feature and will still have to be broken down further.
As a Knight I want a shield so that I can protect myself from the dragon's fire.	User Story (Small)	This story belongs to the Armour Feature, it's small enough to be built during a sprint and meets the INVEST criteria.

Another way of thinking about the hierarchy is as a pyramid, Epics on the top, Features in the middle and User Stories forming the bottom. It could look like this:

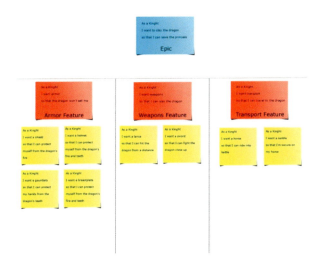

Figure 4.05 User Story Hierarchy

What to avoid when writing User Stories

There are a few things you should do to ensure your User Stories are well written:

1. The User Story should be written from the end users point of view.

Don't make the mistake of writing a User Story that's based on the team's point of view.

So, here's an example of what to avoid:

*"**As a** Knight*
***I want** a shield*
***so that** it can withstand a crush pressure of 1,500 PSI"*

The team will understand this but not the end user.

2. Write the User Story in the end users language.

So, here's an example of what to avoid:

*"**As a** Knight*
***I want a** European Pig Faced Helmet*
***so that** I have full field vision"*

The knight would simply say "I want a helmet I can see out of."

3. There are some words that you should avoid! Here are some examples:

- big, fast, quick, better, less, more

And some buzz words like:

- user experience, value-add, time saver

Basically, we want to be specific. You can define "user experience" by breaking down the elements. So, you could say "I want to complete the form in less than 1 minute".

Replace words like "big" or "more" with numbers like "at least 10" or "three options are shown".

If there any specific circumstances when this User Story might behave differently, add this to the Acceptance Criteria or create a new User Story.

SPOTLIGHT – User Story Splitting

I've seen many teams struggle to split large user stories into small stories in a useful way. They often end up with small vertical slices through their architecture or user interface, they get stories that end up looking more like tasks that fail to meet INVEST or are not "shippable".

Fortunately, story splitting is a skill that can and should be learned by every team member. I've been on teams that have struggled a lot to manage large user stories. When they suddenly started splitting those large stories we began making real progress in the sprints.

There are lots of practical steps you can take to split user stories, and some great tools.

Here's how I look at user stories:

1. *Split by Workflow steps or Happy/Unhappy paths*

2. *Split by Input/Output (i.e. platforms for example desktops, tablets, smartphones)*

3. *Split by Business Rules*

4. *Split by data types (i.e. make the split based on the datatypes that need to be returned or the parameters that should be)*

5. *Split by operations (i.e. CRUD; create, read, update and delete)*

6. *Split by Test Cases*

7. *Split by Roles*

8. *Split by functions – (i.e. account opening, reporting)*

Here's a link to a great poster on User Stories Splitting: http://agileforall.com/resources/how-to-split-a-user-story/

The 3 C's

When writing User Stories, remember the three C's of good story writing:
1. **Conversation** – Have a discussion between the team, customers, stakeholders, and SME's. Also, remember a User Story is really a promise for a deeper conversation leading to mutual understanding by all parties
2. **Card** – write it on an index card using a black sharpie. This will keep the story short and to the point
3. **Confirmation** – create acceptance criteria, using a set technique like Given, When, Then can really help. But don't limit yourself

Acceptance Criteria (aka how we know when the User Story is done)

Every User Story has acceptance criteria; these criteria are used to provide the objectivity required to know when the story has been completed. In other words, these are the tests we will do to see if the User Story works as we expect it.

Acceptance criteria assist the team to think through how a piece of functionality will work from the user's perspective. They remove ambiguity from requirements. Finally, they form the tests that will confirm that the piece of functionality is working and complete.

Here's an example:
As a Knight
I want a shield
so that I can protect myself from the dragon's fire.
Acceptance criteria:
- The shield must be made of steel
- The steel must be able to withstand a heat of 300 degrees
- The knight can only hold a shield if its less than 10 kgs.
- The shield must cover 80% of the knight when held directly in front of him

Non-Functional Requirements

Non-functional requirements are essential. They do not relate directly to the User Story, but to the behavior the User Story describes. They define how well the behavior must perform. Here are some examples; availability, compatibility, performance, maintainability, scalability, and usability. So as an example, Scalability: the degree the User Story is likely to grow or evolve to handle increased amounts of work.

Now you could write your non-functional requirements as User Stories like this:

As a System
I want to support concurrent users
so that I manage growth

Or you could just build a simple table to cover the non-functionals and link the appropriate User Stories to the non-functional area:

User Story	Metric/Requirements	Scale	End of Financial Year [XXXX]			Growth (% or #)		
			Must	Plan	Wish	+Year 1	+Year 2	+Year 3
Non-Functioal Area 1 - Performance								
US100, 106, 108	The system will support concurrent users	Users	30	40	60	5%	10%	15%
US099, 201	Login process will complete	Seconds	25	10	5	N/A	N/A	N/A

Figure 4.06 – Non-functional table

Common User Story Mistakes

There are four common errors people usually make when writing User Stories:

1. Too much detail or "I'm writing the solution not the problem". Sometimes even with the best of intentions, we overcomplicate the User Story. Here's an example:

As a Knight
I want to slay the dragon with my lance while riding on my trusty steed
so that I can save the princess, marry her and become King!

By having so much detail we limit the team's ability to solve the problem, for example, is the lance and horse really the best way to slay the dragon? And do we really need to know the knight plans to marry the princess?

2. Too technical. We often confuse a technical task with a User Story. Technical tasks often don't end up with working software. Here's an example:

   As a Blacksmith
   I want a forge capable of heating steel to red hot in 30 minutes
   so that I can make shields and swords.

   It's important to the team to know what tools they need to build the solution. This is definitely a Task as the user is the team, not the customer the knight.

3. No acceptance criteria. Without acceptance criteria, it's impossible for the team to know exactly what to build for. Your testers will also be unable to test the User Story.

4. Replicated requirements. It's easy to replicate functionality for different users when acceptance criteria are a better option. Here's an example:

   As a Premium User
   I want to log-on to the website
   so that I can view the premium content.

   As a Standard User
   I want to log-on to the website
   so that I can view the Standard content.

   A better User Story would be:

   As a Paying User
   I want to log-on to the website
   so that I can view the appropriate content.

   (**Given**) a Premium User
   (**When**) you log-on
   (**Then**) the Premium Content is viewable
   (**Given**) a Standard User
   (**When**) you log-on
   (**Then**) the Standard Content is viewable
   (**Given**) a Non-member
   (**When**) attempts to log-on
   (**Then**) no content is viewable

This User Story and its acceptance criteria provides more information and the business needs without repetition.

Examples of User Story Splitting

Here are a few examples of how a User Story can be split:
As a PC user
I want to back-up my entire hard drive
so that my data is available if my PC fails.

This is an epic and is too large for an agile team to complete in one sprint, it is split into multiple smaller user stories before it is worked on. The epic above could be split into dozens (or possibly hundreds), including these:
As a PC user
I want to start a one-off backup commencing immediately
so that I can complete a backup

This is an example of a "Workflow" split, the story only deals with a manually commenced backup. Further user stories could include; success messages when the backup is complete, error messages when there is not enough storage space available or stories managing setting up backups to occur in the future.

As a PC user
I want to select a destination folder for the backup
so that I know where the backup will be saved

This is an example of "Inputs/Outputs" as its describing were the file will be output.

As a PC user
I want to back up the operating system only
so that I have a restore point for the operating system

This is an example of a "business rules" split.

As a power PC user
I want to specify files or folders to backup based on file size, date created and date modified
so that I can control the types of files that are available if my PC fails

This is an example of a split by "roles". In this case, we have a "power PC user" who has different needs to a "novice PC user" as below. It could also be an example of a split by "data types" or "test cases".

As a novice PC user
I want to set up a recurring backup
so that I don't have to remember to do it

Putting your User Stories in priority order

Your Backlog is now full of User Stories! The next issue is how do you prioritize them? One way is to use MoSCoW.

The MoSCoW process is a simple way to sort the User Stories that form the Product Backlog into a priority order.

MoSCoW stands for:
Must have
Should have
Could have
Won't have

Must Haves are User Stories that must be included to create the MVP (Minimum Viable Product). Must Haves form the core of the scope of work that will need to be delivered.
Should Haves are User Stories that are not critical to the MVP, but are considered to be important and of a high value.

Could Haves are User Stories that are "nice to have." They could potentially be included where time and resources are available. However, these User Stories will be the first to be removed from scope if the project is at risk of missing delivery of the MVP.

Won't Haves are User Stories or Features that the Product Owner has requested but are not going to be built. These User Stories or Features may be built in the future but are not part of the scope of the current work.

Realistically, the User Stories need to be spread across the categories, so we avoid ending up with every User Story being listed as a Must Have.

Figure 4.07 – MoSCoW

Here's my recommendation for the split values:
Must have – less than 70% of capacity,
Should have – No more than 20% of capacity,
Could have – No more than 10% of capacity,
Won't have – as they won't be built, there is no limit needed.

If you're Must Haves exceed 80% of the total capacity, there will be no flexibility and little contingency if something goes wrong. There will most likely be some Must Haves that we decide won't be built. By having a number of User Stories in the Should and Could have categories, we create flexibility as we can choose to move them up in priority.

Agile embraces change and that means we can't have every User Story prioritized as a Must Have. But what do you do when the Product Owner thinks every User Story is a Must Have?

This is a problem I've faced a number of times. I've managed it by using these three processes:
1. User Story Mapping – what is the most basic path to success?
2. Value Mapping – which User Stories add the greatest value?
3. Feasibility – which User Stories are the simplest to build?

This allows the Product Owner to identify User Stories that are a nice to have, think Henry Ford when he decided to produce black model T Fords only in 1914. The greatest value to both Ford and customers was a simple, easy to build a car. The customers understood that by having different colors for the Model T it would make it more expensive to build. The single color was cheap in cost and very durable. It also simplified the production line.

Grooming your User Story Backlog

The reason you groom your User Stories is to make sure that only relevant and appropriate stories remain in the Backlog.

Remember Agile projects are not like waterfall projects! In waterfall, you create a lot of complex documents that age badly! In Agile the Backlog is a dynamic body of information that changes as your project moves ahead. You will uncover issues some good, some bad that will result in changes.

The Backlog will contain User Stories that have not been fully elaborated, some stories will need to be broken into smaller chunks, others may be "scope creep". This is where estimating and providing a priority really adds value. Remember in Agile we are looking to deliver the MVP (Minimum Viable Product).

So, should you have a formal Backlog Grooming Meeting? I believe yes.

Your grooming should:
1. Write new User Stories and Acceptance Criteria
2. Remove User Stories that are no longer needed
3. Add new User Stories that are required due to limitations or decisions made in prior sprints
4. Update the priority of the User Stories
5. Allow the team to ask questions about the User Stories
6. Allow the team to split User Stories into doable chunks
7. Provide estimates

The benefit of a constant grooming process is that the team has a better understanding of the requirements.

Some grooming tips:
1. Always have your Product Owner at the meeting
2. Have the whole team at the grooming (i.e. including the testers!)

3. Have Technical Support (Architects, Tech Leads, and Customer Experience Leads)
4. In the meeting room have:
    - A whiteboard
    - Post-it notepads
    - the project Personas
    - Customer Journey Maps/Customer Experience documents
    - Planning Poker Cards or Smartphone Planning Poker Apps
5. Remember to be consistent when writing User Stories and developing Acceptance Criteria. Grooming is an opportunity to improve poorly written stories or stories that have little or no acceptance criteria. Acceptance Criteria are needed before the team does any estimates!
6. Set the number of User Stories to be reviewed or Story Points value. This is the time when you can break down User Stories that are too big (i.e. Epics)
7. Time Box the meeting, if you have multiple Product Owners make sure you split the time appropriately
8. Everyone should participate, change roles in the meeting frequently. The reason for this is you don't want all your stories to be written by the Scrum Master!
9. If you have to get technical feedback from stakeholders who are not Product Owners do this outside of the Backlog Grooming. This is so the meeting is not taken over explaining the process, or managing stakeholders scope creep ideas!
10. And most importantly schedule the Backlog Grooming session to support and improve the next Sprint Planning meeting

Backlog Grooming is the key to having a constant supply of quality User Stories for Sprint Planning.

User Story Writing Tips

Keep it simple

Write simple and concise stories that avoid confusing or ambiguous terms. Your User Stories should be easily understood by the whole team.

Write collaboratively

A User Story is basically a communication tool. It's designed to allow you to have more detailed conversations.

I've used the "three amigos" approach, where the Business Analyst, Tester, and Developer work together to better define the User Story and the Acceptance Criteria. However, it's generally best to have the whole team available and any SME guests.

Use INVEST
Following the INVEST process is a good idea as it was designed to create quality User Stories.

Use MoSCoW
Use MoSCoW to prioritize your User Stories. You should prioritize all your User Stories. Without some form of priority, you'll have issues!

Use Personas to build stories
Personas are a fictional representation of the User. This means you have some insights into what the User does/wants/thinks. This will assist you expanding the User Stories to meet the needs of different Users.

So, for example, you may have a Persona where the customer has a lot of experience with your product, a different Persona will cover Users who have no understanding of the product.

Split User Stories when possible
Splitting User Stories early makes life a lot easier. It's a lot better to have a lot of small User Stories than a few really big ones. Big User Stories are hard to estimate and plan into a sprint.

Always have Acceptance Criteria
All User Stories must have Acceptance Criteria. How will you know it's been successfully built? There are lots of different ways to write Acceptance Criteria; any method will do as long as the Product Owner, Developers and Testers can understand them.

A picture is worth a thousand words
User Stories are usually written; however, you can draw it, screenshot it or white board the story. I've developed User Stories that are simply a screen shot of the web page with some things crossed out, buttons crudely added in and comments directly where they relate to the story. If you can take a picture or make a picture do it!

Visible and Accessible
Your User Stories need to be visible and accessible to the whole team. Having an Agile board is a good start. The Customer Experience team will help out here with designs, flows, and customer testing. Have the Acceptance Criteria visible as well, use a process, or system that everyone can access.

Empower the team to make decisions
Requirements emerge and evolve as the project happens. Agile teams must be empowered to make decisions, cooperation, collaboration, and communication is the key.

User Stories will change, remember that's OK. Just make sure that the team is aware of it!

Definition of Ready
User Stories that are "Ready" should be clear, concise, have Acceptance Criteria so it can be tested and most importantly be actionable. Each team should list out the what makes a User Story "Ready". This should be up as a

poster so everyone knows what is needed. I remember seeing a Definition of Ready where the last item was "Dave must have read the text!". It turned out that Dave was the only member of the team that spoke French, the language being used in the interface!

5 ESTIMATING

Estimating or "How big are your User Stories"

Finally, you need to estimate how much effort it will take to build the User Story. We call this process User Story Estimation. It's also important to remember if the content of a User Story is changed in any way it needs to be re-estimated!

The estimate needs to include the building of the User Story, and the testing of the User Story within the Sprint.

The most common form of estimation is Story Point. This process uses a set standard to size the User Stories. Usually, this is expressed in the form a point.

Let's look at an example:

As a Knight
I want a shield
so that I can protect myself from the dragon's fire.

Acceptance Criteria:
- The shield must be made of steel
- The steel must be able to withstand a heat of 300 degrees
- The knight can only hold a shield if it's less than 10 kgs.
- The shield must cover 80% of the knight when held directly in front of him

If your blacksmith believes he can make the shield in about 4 hours. Your tester will then need to check if the shield can withstand the heat, weight it and finally check against the Knight to see if it covers 80% of his body. This will take 2 hours.

Now that we know it will take a total of 6 hours to build and test the shield, we can use it to make relative estimates for other User Stories.

So, we could say that the shield User Story is a "Small". We can then look at other User Stories and say they are either bigger or smaller than the build a shield User Story.

User Story Estimation Process: Note it usually takes 2-3 minutes for each User Story to be estimated.
Steps:

1. Distribute decks of cards with Fibonacci numbers (1, 2, 3, 5, 8, 13, 21...) or T-shirt sizes (XS, S, M, L, XL, XXL) to each participating team member. Or use a Smartphone App.
2. Present the User Story to the team by reading it allowed.
3. Have the team discuss the User Story, allowing developers and testers to ask questions.
4. Ask each team member to select a card from his or her deck, representing the number of story points he or she thinks the User Story requires (relative to past User Stories).
5. Once all the members have selected their cards, ask everyone to reveal their chosen number at once, and ask outliers to discuss on how they arrived at their estimates. You may be tempted to use the "Fist of Five" method. This is where the voting is done by holding up your hand with the number of fingers representing the value. I've found that what often happens is people change their minds when they see other people's choice. This often leads to the "Team Leader" leading the team as no one what's to be seen to disagree! Having a card or smartphone app removes the "quick change of mind" problem.
6. Agree on a story size based on the discussion.
   - For all user stories, determine the worst case, most likely, and best case scenarios for the estimates.
   - If discussions extend beyond the defined 2-3 minutes or everyone can't agree, repeat steps 3 and 4, keeping in light new information revealed during the discussion(s). Estimates typically converge after 2-3 rounds of discussion.

Non-points cards

Symbol	Meaning
∞	Infinity – too big
?	Need more information
☕	Let's take a break

Fibonacci Story Points

Story Points	Bucket
1	Smallest
2	Small
3	Medium
5	Medium-Large
8	Large
13	Very Large
21+	Epic

T-shirts sizes

Size	Bucket
XS	Smallest
S	Small
M	Medium
L	Large
XL	Extra-Large
XXL	Epic

Andrew R. Brien

6 HIGH LEVEL USER STORY WORKSHOPS

Sometimes it's quite difficult to figure out where to start. There are however some simple strategies that you can use to help you manage the first workshop to get requirements.

While generally you can look at it from a top down or bottom up or some combo of both these are the ones I use:
1. People, Process, System
2. Lifecycle (Planning and Research, Product Discovery, Purchasing, Fulfilment, Servicing)
3. Themes vs. Features
4. Used Case

People, Process, System

You can look at the problem from the three core perspectives of the *People* (Customers, Users, and Support), *Process* (such as Sales, Support, Closure), and *Systems* (such as CRM or Core systems, linked systems and manual processes such as data transfer). This can be helpful so long as the workshop can be time-boxed to cover each perspective. There is also the option to look at the process either "top down" or "bottom up". Meaning you could look at the process from the top, meaning the goals or the bottom meaning the processes that exist.

Lifecycle

Following the lifecycle from either the Customer or your Users perspective can really help you understand the requirements. It's also very visual and linear which can help. It can also highlight issues that the team may not have thought about because it is outside the existing process. So, looking at how your customer researches the product can assist in how we onboard or sell to them.

Themes vs. Features

Usually, when you start a project you have an idea of the themes and features you want to deliver. So, you can look at how they interact and use that as a starting point for requirements.

Here's a simple example; you may be building a new website some of the themes may be; Sales, Branding, Communication. The Features could be; Home Page, Products, Contact Us.

You can now look at how the themes interact with the features so that you can say; Home Page – includes Branding but not Sales.

Used Case

A Use Case is a list of pre-determined actions or steps defining the interactions between an "Actor" (such as a Customer or Customer Service Officer) and a system to achieve a goal.

If you have a set of existing Used Cases they can be a great starting point for new requirements.

You can use these in combination to get better coverage. So, you can look at the requirements from a Lifecycle and Themes vs. Features point of view at the same time.

7 TEMPLATE USER STORY CARDS

User Story cards are vital to any Agile project. There's no set rule on the format of the cards but if you're starting out you may want to have template cards. I've created two printable template cards. The cards have INVEST and MoSCoW built in as a reminder!

When ever you are writing or grooming User Stories you may forget to use INVEST and MoSCoW! So, I have developed "Cheat Sheets" on INVEST, MoSCoW, Epics/Features/User Stories and Grooming which are the same size as a User Story card.

You can cut them out of the book as well!

Title: _____

As a ....

I want ....

so that ....

Points: _____

INVEST

Independent

Negotiable

Valuable

Estimatable

Small

Testable

Andrew R. Brien

Intentionally Blank

User Stories Applied

Title: _____ Points: _____

As a ....

I want ....

so that ....

MoSCoW

☐ Must ☐ Should ☐ Could ☐ Won't

Andrew R. Brien

Intentionally Blank

Cheat Sheet - Epics/Features/User Stories

User Story hierarchy; Epics, Features, User Stories

Epics – Very large (Whole project scope)
Features – Medium (a few sprints)
User Story – Small (able to be built during a sprint)

Written as:
As a <user type>
I want <functionality needed>
As that <desired outcome>
Remember all User Stories need to have Acceptance Criteria.

Andrew R. Brien

Intentionally Blank

Cheat Sheet – User Story Grooming

- Have the whole team available
- The Product Owner must attend
- Break down user stories that are too big (i.e. Epics)
- Improve User Stories that are poorly written
- Add acceptance criteria
- Remember to use INVEST when writing new stories
- Use MoSCoW to priorities
- Remove User Stories that are no longer needed
- Map dependences

Andrew R. Brien

Intentionally Blank

8 IMAGE, FIGURES AND TOOLS LIBRARY

Throughout this book, there are photos and figures that help explain Agile and User Stories. To help you out I've made all of them available to you to use. In addition, I've added some tools and templates as well.
To have the electronic copies emailed to you register your copy of this book at www.andrewbrien.com/UserStories

Images available:
- 1.01 Agile Big Picture Overview
- 2.01 Waterfall vs. Agile
- 2.02 Agile vs. Waterfall: Risk vs. Business Value Delivered
- 2.03 What the Business Wants
- 2.04 What the Business Gets - Waterfall
- 2.05 What the Business Gets - Agile
- 2.06 Burn Down Chart
- 2.07 The Agile Umbrella
- 2.08 Core Agile Practices
- 3.01 Create your Product Backlog
- 3.02 Vision Box (image only)
- 3.03 Onion Chart
- 3.04 Lean Canvas
- 3.05 Why and How Now vs. Why and How Future Model
- 3.06 SWOT
- 3.07 Workshop group

3.08   Product Owner
4.01   I'm glad we agree
4.02   I'm glad we actually agree
4.03   A Knight's User Story
4.04   Taking a boulder up a hill
4.05   User Story Hierarchy
4.06   Non-functional table
4.07   MoSCoW

All images are available as PNG for immediate use, and SVG (Scalable Vector Graphics) which can be edited in Adobe Illustrator or the open source program Inkscape (you can download Inkscape for free at https://inkscape.org/en/).

Tools:

Why and How Now vs. Why and How Future Model	Word/PDF
SWOT	Word/PDF
Fibonacci Story Points and T-shirts Sizing Table	Word
Stakeholder Onion Chart	Word/PDF
Vision Box template	PDF
Lean Canvas	PowerPoint
User Story Card - INVEST	Image
User Story Card - MoSCoW	Image
Cheat Sheet - Epics/Features/User Stories	Image
Cheat Sheet - User Story Grooming	Image

9 AGILE DICE

When you first start out writing Agile User Stories you may forget some of the more complex ideas. To help you out and make the process a little more fun I've used dice.

User Story Value Dice – Sometimes it's hard to figure out if the User Story is adding value for the customer. You can use User Story Value Dice to ask the following key questions:
- Does the User Story save the customer time?
- Does the User Story make the customer money?
- Does the User Story save the customer money?
- Does the User Story create an opportunity for the customer?
- Does the User Story complete a step to a goal that the customer has?
- Does the User Story inform the customer?

If your User Story does not do any of the above is it still a good story?

Dice faces shown (two rows of three):
- Save Time | Make Money | Save Money
- Create an opportunity | Step to a goal | Inform

INVEST Dice - Sometimes it's difficult to remember the INVEST process. So having a dice can be of benefit! Used this to help the team understand what to write better User Stories by testing randomly using INVEST.

Dice faces shown (two rows of three):
- Independant | Negotiable | Valuable
- Estimatable | Small | Testable

User Story Splitting Dice - User Story splitting can be difficult at first. Using dice can help in brainstorming possible splits. The six most common splits I've found are:
- Workflow – split up the steps
- Business Rules – split User Stories within the business rules
- Role – split by different roles (data entry, customer service, customer)
- Functions – i.e. account opening, reporting, closures etc.
- Interfaces – such as operation systems (ISO, Android or Windows) or systems (CRM, Website etc.)

- Operations – using CRUD for example (create, read, update and delete)

www.andrewbrien.com	www.andrewbrien.com	www.andrewbrien.com
Workflow	Business Rules	Roles
www.andrewbrien.com	www.andrewbrien.com	www.andrewbrien.com
Fuctions	Interfaces	Operations

I believe writing User Stories should be fun! So use any tool you can to make it easy like dice!

10 GLOSSARY

Acceptance Criteria – Forms part of the User Story. They are the list of desired out comes that are needed for the functionality to work. Think of it as the stuff that must happen for the User Story to be complete. They are often written in the "Given, When, Then" format.

Agile Board – The Agile Board is a visual tool that shows the team which User Stories are being worked on. It normally runs left to right, with the following headings; Sprint Back Log, Build, Test, Approval and Done.

Automated Testing Tools – Software tools used by testers to allow for bulk test cases to be processed. Often used to complete regression testing.

Blockers – Blockers are issues or problems that the team faces that are stopping User Stories from moving to the "done" column.

Burn Down Chart – A burn down chart is a visual representation of work left to do versus time remaining in the sprint. The outstanding work, usually listed as User Story Points is often on the vertical axis, with time along the horizontal.

Business Justification – Business Justification demonstrates the reasons to complete the User Story. It answers the question "Why is this User Story being completed?"

Business Requirements – Business Requirements define what must be delivered to complete the project. Epics, Features and User Stories along with non-functional requirements make up the Business Requirements in an Agile project.

Colocation – Colocation is having the Agile Team members located and working in the same workplace. This allows for the team members to better communicate, collaborate and make decisions.

Continuous Improvement – An Agile approach in which the team learns from experience and constantly keeps improving the process.

Daily Standup Meeting – The Daily Standup Meeting is a short, usually no more than 15 minutes long team meeting. It is intended as a status meeting where the following three key questions are asked:
1. What have you done since the last meeting?
2. What do you plan to do today?
3. What blockers if any are you currently facing?

Dependencies – Dependencies are issues that link tasks and require prior tasks to be completed in a set order. Example; Before you can create the link button you need to have the other web pages address.

Discovery – Discovery is the process the Agile team undertakes to understand the business problem in detail. It usually involves team members working with the Product Owner and SME's to understand the needs of the customer.

Demos – See Show Case.

Epics – Epics are high-level User Stories that need to be broken down into smaller stories.

Estimating – Estimating is the process of working out how much effort it will take to build the individual User Story.

Fist of Five – Fist of Five is a simple visual voting process. The team needs to vote in a range from 1 to 5. The team, all at the same time put their hand up with one to five fingers out representing the points each team member this the story is worth.

Grooming – Grooming is the process of preparing or reviewing work items or User Stories. Grooming is the process of expanding on the item and having it ready for the next step in the process.

Hardening Sprint – The Hardening Sprint is close to the end of the development period where System Integration Testing (end to end testing) is completed.

Increment – See Sprint.

MoSCoW Prioritization – MoSCoW is a simple method of prioritizing User Stories into groups (Must have, Should have, Could have and Won't have).

MMP – MMP (Minimum Marketable Product) is the term used to describe the minimum we could build to realistically go to market and sell our product. For example, we could release a website with just the Home Page and Contact Us pages, but our customers would expect more.

MVP – MVP (Minimum Viable Product) is the term used to describe the minimum we can build to meet the customer's needs.

Planning Poker – A simplified voting process where the team has "cards" that list values. The Cards are used for the team to vote on the amount of effort needed to build the User Story.

Product Backlog – The Product Backlog is the master list of User Stories for the project. Usually, only the User Stories not yet built or in a Sprint Backlog are maintained in the Product Backlog.

Product Owner – Is the key stakeholder for the team. They are the representative of the business and make all the key decisions.

Refactoring – Refactoring is the process of restructuring existing computer code without changing the functionality it delivers. The process is completed to improve the code and make it easier to maintain.

Release Planning – Release planning is the process of determining what scope will be delivered. As Agile allows for working software to be delivered in small increments over time you need to plan that delivery.

Retros – Retros short for Retrospectives is a time-boxed review meeting. During the meeting, the team talks about what happened during the last sprint. It is part of the continual improvement process, with the objective of improving the way the team works.

Scrum board – see Agile Board.

Scrum Master – The Scrum Master is a core team member. They are a facilitator for the team managing the Agile ceremonies and helping the team manage blockers.

Scrum of Scrums Meeting – The Scrum of Scrums Meeting occurs when you have more than one team working on the same code. It is a repeat of the Daily Standup Meeting but for the Scrum Masters of each team. This meeting is to allow all the teams to get an update on the total work in progress.

Show case – The Show case is a core Agile ceremony completed at the end of each sprint. Its purpose is to demonstrate the working software to the product owner and stakeholders. It is a method of getting feedback and present an inspect-and-adapt opportunity for course correction.

Spike – A Spike is a short time-boxed investigation the team undertakes to see if a feature or functionality can be built. Spikes occur when the team is asked to build something that they have not done in the past. At the end of the Spike, the team confirms if they can build it and how long it will take.

Sprint – A time-boxed period where the team builds the User Stories. Usually a period of 10 working days but can be up to 20 working days.

Sprint Backlog – This is the list of approved User Stories to be completed within the Sprint.

Sprint Deliverables – The Sprint Deliverables are the functionality or items that will be delivered at the end of the sprint.

Sprint Planning – Sprint Planning is the process of determining which Backlog items (User Stories) will be taken into the sprint and get built.

Tasks – Often the team will break up the User Story into a series of smaller "tasks". These tasks are then completed to build the full User Story. For example, if you were building a web page tasks could include; Create HTML page, Save in Working folder, Copy images, Code page.

Time boxing – Time boxing is the process of limiting the amount of time spent on a task. This is done by deciding upfront how long we can spend on the process.

Technical Debt – is the term used to describe the rework that will need to be completed by choosing a simpler or easier solution. For example, if we continue to develop code for a system that will be replaced shortly instead of building in the new system we are creating Technical Debt.

User Story Cards – User Story Cards are simple visual records of the User Story that are placed on the Agile Board. They can be real paper cards or electronic cards in Rally or JIRA.

User Story Mapping – User Story Mapping is the process of arranging your stories into a useful visual model. This model allows you to understand how the User Stories create the customer journey. Additionally, it can highlight the MMP and MVP.

Value stream mapping – Value-stream mapping is the process for analyzing the current state and designing a future state for the series of events that take a product or service from its beginning through to the customer.

Velocity – Velocity describes the rate at which the team is completing User Stories, usually as User Story Points. So, if the team completes 10 User Story Points in a Sprint this is their Velocity.

11 INDEX

3 C's	34
Acceptance Criteria	34
Agile Umbrella	12
Burn Down Chart	11
Common User Story Mistakes	35
Core Agile Practices	17
Definition of Ready	41
Epics	31
Estimating	43
Failing fast	11
Features	31
Fibonacci Story Points	45
Grooming your User Stories	39
High level workshops	47
Industry bodies and Organizations	12
INVEST	29
Lean Canvas	23, 26
Manifesto	15
Misconceptions	19
MoSCoW	37
Non-functionals	34
Onion Chart	23
Prioritizing	37

Product Backlog	22
Product Owner	25
Risk Management	8
Shared understanding	28
Speed to market	8
SWOT	24
Technical Practices	19
Test and Learn	14
Transparency	11
T-shirt Story sizes	45
Used Case	48
User Story Splitting	33, 36
Vision	22
Why and How Now vs. Why and How Future Model	24

ABOUT THE AUTHOR

Andrew Brien has over 18 years of experience in IT projects in the finance and lending industry in Australia and New Zealand. He is currently the Lead Business Analyst for Westpac Banking Corp Consumer Digital in Sydney Australia. Where he manages a team of 28 Business Analysts.

Qualifications:

Certified Scrum Master – Scrum Alliance

Certified SAFe Practitioner – Scaled Agile Academy

Certified Agile Professional - ICAgile

Made in the USA
Monee, IL
12 November 2019